The Budgeter's Bible: 27 Techniques for Spending Less than $1,000 A Month

Disclaimer and Terms of Use: Effort has been made to ensure that the information in this book is accurate and complete, however, the author and the publisher do not warrant the accuracy of the information, text and graphics contained within the book due to the rapidly changing nature of science, research, known and unknown facts and internet. The Author and the publisher do not hold any responsibility for errors, omissions or contrary interpretation of the subject matter herein. This book is presented solely for motivational and informational purposes only.

Table of Contents

Introduction

Some would call living on a budget frugal, while others (those that are smart) would call it planning ahead, and living responsibly. What a lot of people don't realize, generally at a young age as a matter of fact, is that living on a budget is something that DOES take time, teamwork for those that are married, and self-control. I can't sit here and tell you that this book holds all the answers. What I can tell you is that I have lived on both sides of the fence. I grew up the adopted only child with two parents whom cared for me, put a roof over my head, food in the kitchen and gave me all the love in the world. With that came little "want" for anything. Meaning, yes I was a spoiled only child.

Now, in my thirties, grown with six children, one amazing grandchild and a spouse who works in civil service I can tell you I can tell you it has taken blood sweat and tears to own the home (and pay the mortgage that comes with it) we come home to every evening. To be blessed to cook in the kitchen that holds the food to feed the five mouths that still live under our roof. Truth be told, I want to share my story, and share these tips in the hopes that someone can learn from my mistakes, selfishness and well, vulnerability.

Throughout the book you are going to read about 50 different tips for living on a budget. A few different budget templates and a few suggestions for online budgeting programs, both free and some that do ask for a monthly service (and yes you have to budget those as well).To start you are going to read about the first 50 tips and suggestions to changing your lifestyle, and living with financial freedom.

Breakfast on the go

1. First meal of the day- Well first of all we know that the first meal of the day is the most important, with that, I want to say that you can eat a healthy breakfast from home, on a budget. IF you eat at home before you leave in the morning you won't be tempted to stop at the donut shop or Starbucks on your way to the office. Saving you on average $8-10 (Remember this amount later) *see more recipes in the recipe sections

Here are a few Breakfast recipes:

Peanut Butter Granola

*Filling and something you can eat on the go, will burn throughout the day keeping you full longer, helping curb those afternoon cravings which also keeps you from pulling into that drive-thru on the way home from work. (Avg. cost $2 per serving)

Ingredients:

- ½ C creamy peanut butter
- ½ C syrup
- ¼ C canola oil
- ½ tsp salt
- 3 C rolled oats
- 1 C roasted peanuts
- Yogurts and berries

Directions: Preheat your oven (you can make this the night before) and combine everything but the yogurt and berries and fold onto baking sheet and bake at 35-40 minutes let cool. Pour evenly throughout 3-4 cups and layer with berries, then yogurt. Store in the fridge, and grab on the way out the door every morning.

Morning Smoothie

These smoothies are easy to make and go great in a cool thermos. If you are looking for something to take along to work in the summer, it only takes about 7 minutes to make and you are out the door. No need to stop at your favorite Julius store. Save yourself that $6 every morning.

Ingredients:

- 1 frozen mango
- ½ C skim milk
- ½ C plain yogurt
- 1 T agave nectar
- Ground ginger

Directions: Puree everything in your blender and pour into cooler cup with a lid and out the door you go! Only about $3 per serving

Green Toast

This may not be the best 'on the go' breakfast, but fat of the matter is it is something you can eat before you leave the house, and something that honestly, is great on the budget as well. $1 per serving

Ingredients:

- 1-2 slices of bread
- 1 avocado, sliced
- 1 T olive oil
- 1 tsp. lemon juice
- Red pepper flakes

Directions: Really simple, make your toast, spread the avocado over the toast. Dabble with lime juice and red peppers, and enjoy.

Special Occasions

Christmas and birthdays are something that we all have in our lives, as well as Easter, New Years, and a few others in between. It is ok to splurge a little, but only if you know how to live within your means. Which is what this whole book is really about. That one tip that took me so long to figure out is really rather simple. Live within your means.

Here are a few tips and tricks to save for those annual gift giving holidays:

2. Greeting Cards, this is something that has turned into a dying breed, but it is something that you can find alternative means for. Did you know on average families spend about $150 a year on Christmas cards? Between the stamps, family photos, envelopes, etc. etc. you are spending a lot of money for something that is set on a mantle (maybe) than thrown in the trash a few weeks earlier. Does this seem like a good investment to you? Try virtual Christmas cards.

3. Wrapping paper is something you really can't avoid, and I will tell you from personal experience, it is something that I have wracked my brain for years with. What can I do to save money on paper that looks pretty, gets torn up and set in the trash? This is something that you can't get around. If you're going to do presents, than you have to wrap them SOMEHOW. Well, proudly, I can tell you I have a few suggestions.

- Gift bags are great for the adults, and you can do this for the older kids if they don't rip into the bags. After gifts are given and opened you can reuse them. You can go to a dollar store for tissue paper, or just tape the bags together. I have used the same bags 3-4 years in a row. Save a lot of money this way. See the section on the top 101 things you can buy at a dollar store.
- Use old Christmas cards for tags, this is a lot of fun too
- Use material as wrapping (incorporate this into their gift budget) Use a team logo, pattern they like etc.

4. Homemade decorations are a lot of fun for the whole family. No need to spend hundreds of dollars on decorations when you can make your own. Or using things from nature... Berries, pinecones, etc.

5. Clearance- Go to the store AFTER Christmas for next year's tree, decorations etc.
6. Christmas Budget- This is a holiday that most celebrate, and if you don't, that's fine just take the one tradition that you spend the most on each year giving to others. Now I'm not going to sit here and tell you to "turn into Scrooge" just the opposite. For me it took nearly a decade of being married, and living on a budget, and a few embarrassing moments of returning overly expensive gifts later...heart breaking and humiliating I may add. You can still have an amazing Christmas with great gifts, and food, without going broke or taking out loans. Ok, so set a budget for the year for Christmas. You should be planning for NEXT YEARS Christmas for this year's Christmas. Start an envelope ahead of time with a designated amount, and do not go over it. Whatever you have come fall, that is what you spend.

Groceries

This is a topic I can proudly say I have taken a lot of time to work on. This is something that I have sweated over, struggled with, and finally am comfortable with. There are several different ways to save money on a budget. With this in mind, I have tried a few different things, and have found that what works for one family may not be the best option for the next. So, here is where I want to start.

7. Coupons- This is something that everyone should be familiar with, and depending on your age you probably remember your parents clipping coupons sitting at the kitchen table for hours while you helped, most likely. Well now you can get your coupons online. Pick the ones that you want, and print them off. Or you can use promo or coupon codes that you give the checkout girl at the register. Me personally, I have always stuck with coupons that I can see, hold and print. I don't like to take the chance of the promo code not working. Technology is great, but not when it could potentially come between my saving a few dollars or not.

8. Use pricematcherz.com this is a great site, it may not be available in all areas, but it does allow for you to see what other stores are offering as far as sale prices, or everyday prices. Stores like Walmart and Target do offer price matching. Simply print off the list for your area, highlight the items that you are needing to get, and make sure that you are getting the best prices for your items. On a personal note, I do my price checking before I go to the store, take a pen and min I sticky notes and add the prices on my sticky notes BEFORE I go, tag them to my list, and use that to "mark off" what I have already gotten. This way, I know what I have in my cart, and can "check" it off my list. NOW take it from me, you want a backup list with prices, sticky notes don't ALWAYS stick to the items... so it's good to have that list just in case.

9. Dollar store- this is something that you want to pay attention to, I have a list at the end of this book regarding different things that you can get at a dollar store INSTEAD of your traditional retail store, saving you HUNDREDS of dollars a year.

10. Choose a budget and stick to it- This is something I had a very hard time with, thinking well I'm not feeding them enough, or I

need to buy this instead of that etc. Compromising on a budget is not something that you can do or should do. With that in mind I learned that finding a meal plan and sticking to it is best. I change it up seasonally. I have added a sample winter list below, all this can be purchased for under $100 a week in the Midwest and almost all of the ingredients are something that can be prince matches.

Monday- Chili in slow cooker $6
Ingredients: 1 lbs. ground beef, 1 can tomatoes and chilies, chili powder packet, I can chili beans

Tuesday- Lasagna $10
Ingredients: 1 lbs. ground beef, 1 can spaghetti sauce, No bake Lasagna noodles, shredded cheese

Wednesday-Sour Cream chicken $12
Ingredients: 1 lbs. chicken breast, sour cream, 1 can family size cream of chicken soup, egg noodles, I package French onion soup

Thursday- Spaghetti $6
Ingredients: 1 lbs. ground beef, 1 package spaghetti noodles, spaghetti sauce

Friday- Smothered Pork chops $10
Ingredients: 1 package family pork chops, 1 can cream of mushroom soup, 8 oz. sour cream, potatoes

Saturday $15 Pancakes, Grilled cheese, Roast (breakfast, lunch and dinner)
Ingredients: Pancake mix, milk, bread, cheese, roast dinner package

Sunday $25 BRUNCH, Beef tips and noodles
Ingredients: Beef stew meat, noodles, beef stock and seasoning

11. Deep Freezer- Getting bulk items isn't always going to be the best way to go but owning a deep freeze does allow you to store meat and other frozen items which will cut down on trips to the store.
12. Buy your meat a butcher, and if you have the capabilities buy whole hams in a variety of cuts, as well as beef, pork and chicken. Generally when you buy whole chickens, whole hams, etc. you will get a discount.
13. Over the counter- we all know about the different controversies over medical insurance and Obamacare etc. right now, with that

in mind, buy your vitamins, power shakes etc. online such as amazon, etc. if it is something you can get over the counter, than you will be saving hundreds of dollars MONTHLY.

14. Savings- When you get paid, whether it is weekly, monthly etc. It is important that you have a designated amount that goes to savings every pay period. There is a savings plan for 12 months that allows you to save roughly $1300 a year if followed. See templates and sample budgets for better ideas.

15. Farmers Markets- This goes along with our idea of shopping carefully, buying meat at the butcher etc. this is something that you can do is buy FRESH fruit and vegetables is to save money.

16. Shop around- and we don't mean physically going to different stores. Everything I mentioned in the grocery section can help you with this.

17. ATMS- Do you know how much money you LOSE in atm fee's every year? Go back and look at your transactions over the last year, see how much you have spent on out of network fee's over the last year. You will be shocked, and disgusted! Always use YOUR banks ATM or withdrawal money when you deposit checks etc. It is always good to have cash on hand but you don't NEED to carry more than $100 at any given time.

18. Take your lunch to work or school- this is a lot like my comment and tip on taking your breakfast to go. If you can take your lunch or a school snack with you then you have NO reason to go down that main street where all of the fast food restaurants are.

19. Better insulation- This is something that a lot of homeowners don't stop and think about. There is something about owning a home, and as mentioned earlier, it is nothing closer than a miracle that my family has the home we do, and yes, we do everything we can to make sure the electric bill stays down. There is budget billing that generally is marketed to help you, but the fact of the matter is, that isn't always there to help you. You can set it up, but if you are capable of paying the full amount each month, you need to do this. Otherwise you will have to pay it at the end of the year. You don't want that.

20. Impulse buying- You do your shopping from home, know how much money you need and of course, what you need and nothing

more do not ALLOW YOURSELF to buy ANYTHING that is not on that list.

21. Eat before grocery shopping- This is one of those things that we all do, and that is why impulse buying is so easy, especially if you are hungry. Go in the evening, after dinner.
22. Do you use a dry cleaner? Why? Did you know that most civil servant jobs require a uniform? But do NOT offer clothing allowance? Invest in a $2 bottle of starch, a $15 ironing board and a $20 iron and learn to do it yourself!
23. Homemade cleaning supplies- A lot easier than you may think. Shampoos, conditioners, detergents, cleaners etc. They can last a LONG time. Better than spending $10 on EACH every month or SO. Check out our recipes book on homemade remedies and home cleaner recipes.
24. Do your own repairs-This is something that a lot of you probably already do, but I know we have saved thousands on doing our own automobile repairs. Now, if it is something you don't how to repair and don't feel comfortable doing, this is understandable, but before you dump $200 an hour in service work, look into other options.
25. Use WI-Fi- If you have a data plan on your phone, use free Wi-Fi from home or businesses that offer free Wi-Fi rather than using your data on your plan. This will help cut back on your data usage.

Recipes on a budget

Baked Rigatoni

Ingredients:

- 16 oz. Rigatoni ($1 Barilla)
- 1 lbs. ground beef ($2.98)
- 16 oz. pasta sauce ($2.98 Ragu)
- 1 T minced garlic ($4.98 for 8 oz. container)

Directions: Cook your ground beef, in skillet, and boil noodles in a sauce pan, drain grease from beef and stir in pasta sauce. Drain noodles and combine the two pans and serve warm.

Ingredients:

- Onions (.50)
- Peppers ($1.00 or three)
- 12 oz. can black beans (.68)
- 12 oz. can chicken broth (1.00)
- 12 oz. can tomatoes and chilies (1.29)
- 1 lbs. ground beef ($2.98)

Directions: Use ingredients to make traditional chili, in saucepan. Add ingredients, (cooked beef) and let simmer on stove top for about 12-14 minutes.

Ingredients:

- Red potatoes ($1.29)
- Bag frozen broccoli ($1.29)
- ½ gallon milk ($2.25)
- Shredded cheese ($4)
- Bread crumbs ($1)

Directions: Steam broccoli, heat oven to 375 degrees, add potatoes to saucepan and boil. Simmer and add everything to baking dish cover and bake for 35 minutes.

Veggie Tacos

Ingredients:

- 8 oz. refried beans ($1.50)
- Tortilla shells ($2)
- Salsa ($2.50)
- Lettuce ($.99)
- Maxi blend cheese ($4)

Directions: This is a traditional taco minus the meat. Which could be added for $2.98 for a pound of hamburger.

These are just a few recipes that are out there which allow you to stay within that $1000 budget. Now we have talked about food, holidays and a little bit about saving. But there are a few common core elements that come into the budget:

Rent	$375
Utilities (electric and gas)	$74
Phone	$35
Food	$100
Health Insurance	$66
Car Insurance	$20
Savings for irregular expenses	$100
Entertainment	$100
Gasoline	$100
Miscellaneous	$30
Total	**$1000**

Now this is just a sample budget, but it is a realistic budget. Now I know most don't have the luxury of spending $350 on rent or a mortgage for that matter so you may need to adjust the amounts a little. Check out the 12 month savings chapter for more advice!

Jan

People come into Jan with the idea that this is the year for you to dos something new, for you to take that New Year's resolution and run with it. Well you have to remember to take baby steps. This month you are going to not allow yourself to jump in head first. You know what your budget is going to be, or at least you should BEFORE the first of the year, so you know how to start. This month is about saving and taking things one at a time. NO debt. This month, your step is to use cash, charge NOTHING and cut up ALL of your credit cards. YES ALL OF THEM. Cancel any monthly subscriptions, gym memberships and anything that you pay a monthly premium or payment on. If you don't have the cash to pay for a year in full, than you don't need it.

Feb

Alright, how did you do with month one? Now, as Feb crawls in we want you to take a journal or tablet, whichever you are most comfortable with and write about your month (Jan) what you found hard, what you thought was surprisingly easy etc. With that in mind, it will show you what your spending triggers are, and where you need to add extra attention. So IF you stayed with rule one, you get to treat yourself to one thing. CASH only. And if you have the money to pay your bills for the entire month and have a cushion for your savings, than you can treat yourself to something that is ½ of what you in saving (NOT your savings, you do NOT touch that) Say you have $100 in your RED Savings envelope (for emergencies only) then you may treat yourself to something that is $50. Maybe this is a date night for you and your spouse, a special purse, etc.

March

Now you have been going strong for 60 days or more and you can give yourself a small pat on the back. This is great. This month you should have a little more self-confidence than what you started off with and you need to tell yourself you are worth the hard work and self-control. Show yourself and everyone else that you are worth the respect from others. No loans, no credit cards, self-control.

If you have a career you need to stop and and evaluate where you are in your career and if it is time to look into something else, or request a raise. The reason for waiting until month three for this is you need to see that you are in control of your current finances. What is the point in asking for a raise (more money) if you can't control what you have coming in now? Can't put the cart before the horse.

April

This is the time of year a lot of people start thinking about spring cleaning and what most people overlook is the one area that needs the most clearing out. Your budget. Now four months into your new financial freedom it is important to know where to clear out the unnecessariness. Look at your last 3 months of the budget and see where you can clear out a few expenses that you don't need, areas where you can save a little more and areas where you may need to move around funds. By now you should have a good start on your 6 months' worth of bills savings, your $500 emergency fund, a Christmas savings fund and still be making your bills without any issues. If you find yourself not making the bills on time, stop and look at the core bills, and the luxuries: cable/digital, cell phone bills, clothing, fuel etc. where can you cut loose?

May-June-July

The summer is here and you are half way through your new financial lifestyle. Take the time to save money. That is your goal this month. No extra expenses. Anything family trips, expenses etc. you can set aside for NEXT year and when you have the money then you can decide if that is how you want to spend it. You will find it a lot easier to "spend" money when it isn't in hand, rather than when you have cold hard cash in hand.

August

Start looking into taxes. This is the time to start thinking about tax season. If you pay attention to coming in what's going out financially, then you will be able know exactly what is going on. If you keep receipts, know last year's returns etc. than you should have no issues come tax season, but it is SMART to plan now.

September

Do you have student loans? If so you should be in a position now to start paying them back. We expect that you should be closer to your 6 months' worth of bills, your savings and at a point where you can start working down your debt. Contact the student loan office and see what you can do.

October

Start going for next year. This is where you need to start planning all major expenses for the following year. Plan for any trips, gatherings, replacing any electronics or appliances etc. This is the time to start saving and planning.

November

Start your holiday shopping now, and again no credit cards allowed use cash only. NO lay-away no payments no loans. All cash.

December

Your Christmas or holiday shopping should be different than any other year. Your shopping should be done and this should be the first stress free Christmas you have ever had. Relax, and congratulate yourself. You did it.